Hygiene and Health

Claire Llewellyn

QED Publishing

First published in the UK in 2006 by
QED Publishing
A Quarto Group company
226 City Road
London EC1V 2TT
www.qed-publishing.co.uk

A catalogue record for this book is available from the British Library.

ISBN 1 84538 369 9

Written by Claire Llewellyn
Designed by Susi Martin
Editor Louisa Somerville
Consultant Ruth Miller B.Sc., M.I.Biol., C.Biol.
Illustrations John Haslam
Photographs Michael Wicks

Publisher Steve Evans
Editorial Director Jean Coppendale
Art Director Zeta Davies

Printed and bound in China

Picture credits

Key: t = top, b = bottom, c = centre, l = left, r = right, FC = front cover

Gettyimages Cat Gwynn p12t, Micael Kelly p16, Nancy Ney p18

Words in **bold** are explained

in the glossary on page 22.

Contents

Hooray for health!

It's great to be **healthy**. Healthy people look and feel well.

They have energy to do lots of different things – to work, be **active** and have fun with their friends.

Think about it!

We don't always feel healthy all the time. Think about when you were last ill.

How did you feel? What did you do to make the time pass?

There are lots of things we can do to keep ourselves healthy.

drink plenty of water

get lots of exercise

eat lots of fruit

use suncream when you're outside in hot weather

keep clean

get a good night's sleep

Do it!

What activities do you do each week? Do you ride a bike, sing, play or swim? Make a poster with photos or drawings of yourself to show how active you are!

Staying healthy

What can we do to stay healthy?

We can eat different foods and try to live an active life with lots of fresh air.

water

eggs, fish, meat and cheese

bread, rice and pasta

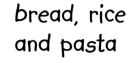

fruit and vegetables

Different foods give you energy, help your body to grow and keep you healthy.

Which of these things help you to stay healthy? Which ones do not?

eating crisps

playing computer games

watching television

eating an apple

playing tennis

playing football

roller skating

Star tip

Our bodies need plenty of water to work well. Try to drink several glasses of water a day.

Do it!

Fruity face

With an adult to help you, make a healthy pudding. Use a banana, satsuma, berries and some lettuce to make a fun face on a plate. Are there other foods you could use?

Germ alert!

Germs are tiny living things in the world around us. We can't see them but some of them can make us ill.

Germs can get onto and into our bodies from the air, from our clothes and from the things we touch.

Germs can live under your fingernails and toenails. Keep nails short and clean.

How do these things help to keep you clean and smelling sweet?

shampoo

scrubbing brush

shower

soap

talcum powder

Watch out!

Washing helps to keep our bodies clean and to get rid of dirt and germs.
● Feet soon begin to smell. Wash them every day!
● Wash your hair at least once a week to get rid of **sweat** and dirt.

Do it!

Draw a fun picture of what you would look (and smell) like if you never washed. What would your friends think of you?

Stop germs spreading

Have you ever caught a friend's cold or had an upset tummy? Germs can spread quickly from person to person, especially on our hands.

Germs can spread from pets. After you touch them, wash your hands.

The best way to stop germs from spreading is to wash your hands before you touch food and after you have been to the toilet.

'Coughs and sneezes spread diseases!'
Germs spread through the air when you cough and sneeze.

Cover your mouth when you cough and use a handkerchief when you sneeze.

Do it!

Take time to wash your hands and nails properly. When you rub them with soap, sing the whole verse of 'Happy Birthday' to yourself.

Yummy or yukky?

Some germs spoil our food and make it bad to eat.

Watch out!

Flies crawl on all sorts of dirt and are good at spreading germs. Never let them land on your food. Cover it or put it away.

You can help to stop this happening by being careful.

Help to keep the kitchen clean by wiping up spilt food and drink after a meal.

Quick quiz!

Which of these foods should be stored in the fridge?

cheese

biscuits

tea bags

pasta

fish

tins of food

meat

Do it!

The last date we can use food is often printed on it. Some foods keep for a day, others last for years. Look at the packaging on different types of food. Can you find the use-by dates?

Tooth talk

We use our teeth to bite and chew – what would we do without them?

Your teeth have to last you all your life. Brushing them daily and going to the dentist will help to protect them.

Star tip

Brush your teeth every morning after breakfast and before you go to bed at night. This gets rid of germs and sugar, and makes your breath smell fresh.

Do it!

You should brush your teeth for about two minutes. How long is two minutes? Use a timer and see!

Ouch! Tooth decay gives you toothache!

Watch out!

The sugar in food harms our teeth and helps to cause **tooth decay**. Try to cut down on sweets, biscuits and fizzy drinks. Choose healthier snacks instead.

Quick quiz!

Which of these foods are bad for your teeth?

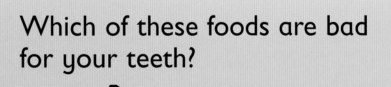

peanuts

lollypop

sweets

bottled water

fizzy drink

apple

biscuits

Whatever the weather

It's good to get outside when we can and breathe in the fresh air.

Before you go out, look at the weather. Is it sunny or cold? Are you properly dressed?

Safety first!

- In cold weather, your body loses heat quickly.

- Wear warm clothes to **protect** yourself from the cold.

Quick quiz! When would you wear or use these? How can they protect you?

Star tip In summer, the sun is strong and can harm your skin. Always put on sun cream, wear a hat and T-shirt, and stay in the **shade** at midday.

socks

sun hat

umbrella

woolly hat

scarf

gloves

raincoat

Do it! Draw a picture of a hot, cold or rainy day. Look through a magazine or catalogue to find people wearing the right clothes for your picture. Cut them out and stick them on your picture.

Taking care

Accidents happen every day and people can get badly hurt. Watch out for danger, and try to keep yourself safe.

If you hurt yourself, tell a grown-up as soon as you can.

Draw a picture of a room in your home. Mark places that you think are a possible danger. How could you stop accidents happening there?

If you cut yourself, wash your skin and cover it with a plaster. This stops germs from getting inside.

- Never pick **scabs**. The germs on your fingers will get into the cut and make it worse.

- If you get stung, put a lump of ice on your skin to help stop the swelling and the pain.

- If you burn your skin, put it in cold water for about 10 minutes and tell a grown-up immediately.

Star tip

If you have an accident always tell a grown-up straight away.

Quick quiz

Many accidents happen at home. How could these be dangerous?

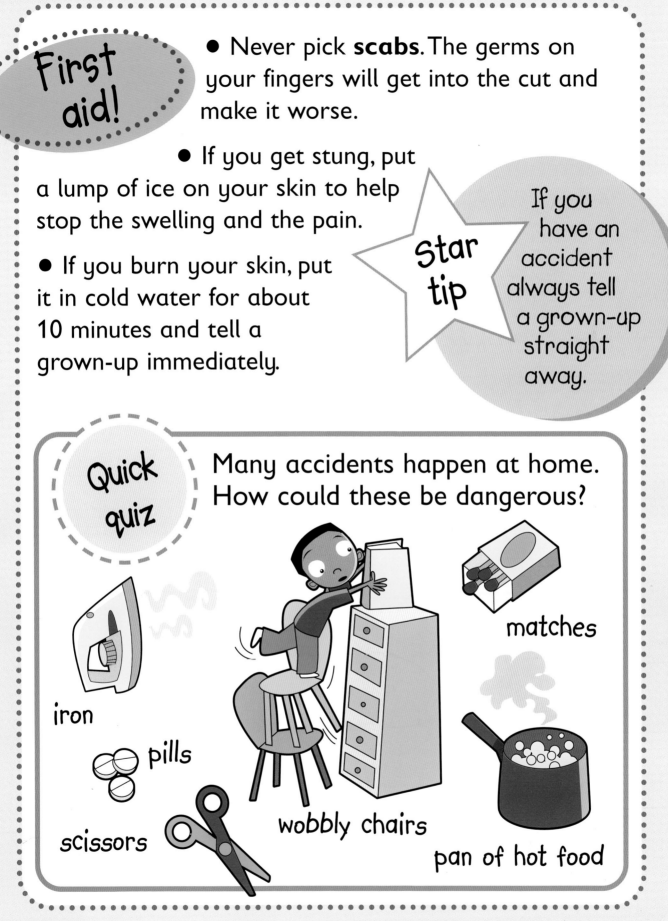

iron

pills

scissors

wobbly chairs

matches

pan of hot food

Night, night!

Our bodies are very busy during the daytime. At night they need to rest.

A good night's sleep helps our body to **recover** and gives us energy for the day ahead.

sleep well!

When you feel ill it's important to get plenty of rest. Rest helps your body to fight the illness and makes you feel better.

Do you ever go to bed too late or have a bad night's sleep? How do you feel the next day?

Do it!

Do we all need the same amount of sleep? Ask your friends, parents and grandparents what time they go to bed and get up.

Work out how long they sleep and show the **results** on a chart. Which age group sleeps the most?

Glossary

accident a bad thing that suddenly happens and hurts someone

active moving around and doing things

germs tiny living things that can spread sickness

healthy fit and well

protect to stop you from being harmed

recover to get back to normal

result what you have found out in a survey

scab a dry crust that forms over a cut while it heals

shade a cool, darker place away from sunlight

sweat the sticky liquid that comes out of your skin when your body is hot. Sweating helps you to cool down

tooth decay when your teeth go bad and rot

Index

Notes
for parents and teachers

- Encourage your children to be more active. Help them to plan a number of 10-minute activity sessions – e.g. learn to skip with a skipping rope, roller skate up and down the path – and to do two of them every day.

- Can the children use a timer or stopwatch to time races between them? As well as running, they could try hopping, or walking backwards, or have a three-legged race. Suggest they try the races again. Can they beat their own best time?

- Visit a supermarket or health food shop and look at all the dried fruits, nuts and seeds. Explain how these are better for the body than sugary biscuits and cakes. Together, try a new healthy snack or create a new pudding.

- Your children could ask their grandparents about what they used to eat when they were young. Were people more or less healthy in those days?

- Discuss the different foods the children eat at mealtimes. Explain how each food helps our body and what it means to have a balanced diet.

- Try out different soaps and shower gels. Which one makes the most bubbles? Which one has the nicest smell?

- Do your children prefer a wash, a shower or a bath? You could conduct a survey of the likes and dislikes of several children. Which is the most popular way of washing?

- Play a memory game based on personal hygiene – e.g. 'Dirty Dan went to the bathroom and brushed his teeth.' 'Dirty Dan went to the bathroom. He brushed his teeth and washed his ears.' 'Dirty Dan went to the bathroom. He brushed his teeth, washed his ears and scrubbed his nails.' Etc.

- Make a fruit salad with your children, explaining about hygiene and safety (e.g. with peelers and knives). Keep everything clean, wash the fruit and keep the food in the fridge until it's time to eat. Wash everything up and put it all away.

- Teeth come in different shapes and sizes. Using books and the Internet, help your children to find out more about them. What jobs do the different teeth do?

- Pay a visit to the dentist or invite one to school. Talk to the dentist about his/her work. Help your children to make a factsheet about good dental care. Sweet foods (in moderation) are not bad in themselves but the sugary residues that get stuck between teeth cause problems.

- Look at some clothes and shoes suitable for summer and winter wear. Discuss the differences between them.

- Ask your children to think of any words that are connected to accidents. They can be fact words, such as 'fire' or 'danger' or words about how accidents make us feel, such as 'hurt' or 'scared'. Can they draw a picture to accompany each word?